FROM THE AUTHOR'S
PRIVATE COLLECTION

FROM THE AUTHOR'S PRIVATE COLLECTION

ERIC AMLING

BIRDS, LLC | AUSTIN, MINNEAPOLIS, NEW YORK, RALEIGH

Birds, LLC
Austin, Minneapolis, New York, Raleigh
www.birdsllc.com

Cover designed by Eric Amling
Interior designed by Michael Newton
Author photo by Erin Albrecht

Cover Image: Bray/Schaible Design Inc.
©1978 THE BED AND BATH BOOK
Terence Conran

Library of Congress Cataloging-in-Publication Data:
Amling, Eric
From the Author's Private Collection/Eric Amling
Library of Congress Control Number: 2015934498

First Edition, 2015
ISBN-13: 9780991429837
Printed in the United States of America

CONTENTS

2010–2015

Some lines that needed to be cut from this book:

Ninety-nine percent of what follows is true

Like mountain water in the form of negotiating streams

I sit on this veranda witnessing a threesome

With time and space and a blimp

Just me and this taciturn bust of Helen Keller

Balled out underneath the sugar moon

Some lines on dysphoria cut from this book:

In 2010 a subliminal mortal prenup took hold of me

I felt my terms of use had expired

In 2012 there was a breach of etiquette

A misnomer that took me far into the evening

Like a polygraph of a satellite

Depicting a protracted landscape contagious and crime wave fantastic

Making you wish for a palindrome life with a decent breeze

Some lines I cut as the author of this book:

The Haitian poet Roumer admires an ass so spectacular

It is like a gorgeous basket brimming with fruits and meat

When I'm out walking I think of this

Rationing an individual thought

To my classified adulteries

I have to dig into a platform of reason

Create a pond in the land of misconduct

Though because of truth I have trouble with its reflections

Some lines on aesthetics cut from this book:

The quiet spectacle of infrared deer

An x-ray of a complicated handshake

Sun-fried eggs on a flotilla of nightshades

Ask me to justify the mood I'm in

The density of my finance identity advancing hysteria

This page weighed down by US mint and human hair

It killed something that's going to need reassembling

Something beautiful, with an underarm tender to the pull

Some lines on incarnation cut from this book:

As an actor portraying chilliness

Standing in the shadows of Hebrew neon

I grasp the origin of my existence

Studying a swan

On the choppy farrago of the bay

So what if I spend hours in the basement with my trains

A portrait of a new omen

In 2015, the author, ruminating into an oyster

Some lines on my character cut from this book:

A video I wish to have the pleasure of making

Where the bookworm fucks then reads for half-an-hour

To put one finger inside you

Slap your ass until you come

Bring you water with a lemon slice

Then select Brian Eno's *Music for Airports*

With a far-off thundercloud crossing our point of view

Outwardly beautiful and inwardly aggressive

Some lines I feel were sacrificed for this book:

With perky music we vacation from the silicone

Not to mention the hidden blues of unisex tennis

In the district of white jazz

Buried in a dragnet of hillsides

Is our waste and our gases

That burn cobalt and satin yellow

Like sixties empires roaring in paisley flames

Some lines on work ethic cut from this book:

Poetry, like cat urine, can ruin the integrity of a room

It can also be a stealthy dominatrix

From the jet-black pussy of a panther, an exact replica

Don't tell the others I'm here please

It's mostly an illicit dream

Sourced from iridescent catacombs

We both should not outlive our acceptance from those closest to us

Keep churning that sphinx on the spit and let it not spoil

HEIR APPARENT

The search for perfection

It's only natural

I close my eyes and put myself in that place

That not lost just physically invisible place

What eyes cannot see the heart cannot grieve at

Every window tinted

A depot of eyelashes pressed to the viewfinder

And there are bright people

And ceremonies to accommodate their advantages

The money has this peach fuzz to it

There are miles of piping to serve the purpose

Of relinquishing ourselves

Considering you are human

The sea, the moon, and a jail in the cattail's sway

I'm taking this plastic flamingo to the shooting range

To relive nightly a besieged leisure

Piecing together a lonely tale of a job, a marriage, and a family that loves you

A party line effete and fearing its children

Ultimately on the other side of the others

Take yourself to a series of offbeat Westerns

Snacking on discontinued sweets

It takes a memorable year to decide

But the picnic was off the chain

I had trusted in something horribly nonexistent

In the gabled barns of self-employment that saw far past the tubing river

With no kettle sludge, no heat lightning

With rodents in the wall that sound like congressional whisper tapes

I accelerate the brain-shaped automobile

Through shires of rain

To little cottages for real tennis

And incomplete origami on the kitchen counter

Obstacles of courtship where life is never safe

You get the blues

A leaking nostril that confronts the world

To vast reaches

Using trinkets to outwit evil

And die the right way

Johnny rolls on his deodorant and checks the calendar for fun

Dominique wears a beige cable-knit sweater

Barbara adds sultry sophistication to a cotton-knit zip-turtle top

Jesús is in dramatic torch light with airbrushed boulders

It takes all of our relationships

all of our ties with the environment to shrink in duration

Not just because of the sexual mechanics of an expensive smelling couple

Modesty is born out of a sense of shame

During the finest epochs

Wearing zone-huggers to bed

Corsets sacrificed to build battleships in the early wars

The climate secondary, the flesh mortified

Torsos with random shoulder hairs

English cleavage, Egyptian cleavage, Sicilian cleavage, Peruvian cleavage

Some kind of systemic vaudevillian act

Where you're reborn as a fantastic rumor

One of the most ancient monuments in the Western Hemisphere

The entrée festooned with a parasol

Consider: clouded ice cube melting through patio chair

On a tarnished afternoon when we still worshipped the food pyramid

With Miss Utica

Miss Schenectady

Sawmill daughters

Heavy action in a pillowed corner of natural light

As immortality produces no art, no lust

Lake water dripping from the undercarriage of a mallard

The firing pistons in the mallard's heart

A swarm of bees moving in the shape of a gavel

In the perimeter of sex gods

Wearing jewels and sipping daiquiris

Geysers and trailers and hoop earrings

Snow falling in a town higher up the mountain

The sound of an engine block's spectacular burst fevers

Today I am a naturalist

Stopping every so often to bite at cool grass blades

Examine a defenseless skeleton

Strain my water through a cloth to avoid the adoring tapeworm

A scratch-off pinned against a brook rock

Golden white pillars of sun on chateaus of aquamarine

Some Native Americans believed consuming gold allowed human levitation

This isn't true, physically

Though freedom still remains monetary

The earlier notion having died with its creator

WHITE NOISE

I'm not interested in driving my convertible
today. There is a small cloud in the sky.
This afternoon will be spent squeezing
a little lemon juice onto an erotic stain
on these cotton pants
looking with pleasure at a high-heeled shoe
covered in dog hair. I can do this
because my money is automatically
exchanged for me. My secrets in plastic.
Secrets that can be most revealing,
like creating a website devoted
to every object in your room.
Every tetra in the fish bowl.
Every capsule of weight gainer.
Then, when there is nothing left to archive
but the sound, you can record the sound
of the room and it sounds like a biologist had
lifted a cage and mice began running through
a field, urinating onto some dry leaves;
it is the softest sound a human ear can hear,
which makes you want to take up arms
against the music of the world. Because when I
listen to the music of the world I put on my
BluBlockers and become a time machine.
Because we are the new ancestors of time.
And when I travel back to the origins of a song
I want to charm it for its secrets.
For the pretty peasant girls who walk in rich attire.
For the gossips in the spas of wherever.

For the ecstasy of crossbreeding
at a government border. And it must be dusk
because the romance of it is overwhelming
and the mistress is overwhelming, and the weight
of age comes with a nobility like good people
toiling in a factory until dusk with nothing else
to know but the sound of labor and of machines
and of a future you and of your secrets
you exchange for another's secrets
and the songs I adore are about them,
about adultery, about a kindness in the pain,
and how the drinks reset the day that is
no longer in a field but a room
with me, my drinks, my obvious themes I address
that repeat through chains of command
like this anthill I know of in a field
where I get down on my knees and scream
as hard as humanly possible just for them
to pick up on my possessed vibrations.
So they become something like me,
some sympathizer.

VELVET REAL TIME

In a pedigree of wildflowers
I reach down to pick up
my magenta piece of gum.
This is the opening thought
to the rest of my life.
Like a transparent diary
the narrator says, "You are like
other people, yet in some ways
you may not like the same foods
as other people."
Here is Amling witnessing
the evolution of the snack chip.
Here is Amling witnessing
commercials with burger zooms.
An academic refugee
sworn to the seductions of taste.
In an empty ashtray I haphazardly
placed my semen, as I minored in Art.
Great amounts of energy consumed
in the production of mental life
had me scared; if zero relevance
looked in a mirror
it would see relevance
stepping out of conjoined horizons
ensuring my vacancy
reducing time to a garnished ingredient.

ILL ESTATES

It's a misdemeanor to threaten the life of a butterfly in Pacific Grove

John Denver's plane hit the water there

His head and body so compromised

The authorities used fingerprints from his DUI for confirmation

Nearby is the strangling weight of chlorine in the air

A neglected sex doll shrinking in the sunlight

You wake in an asymmetrical province unable to find your keys

Some first world problems in the shade of a eucalyptus

The beach; people really get into it

The nerve endings of bikinis

Someone is saying Zen stuff to someone with an engagement ring

It's dangerous to get too autobiographical; there's a radiation to it

These highlight films of you in my mind

I'd apply an artificial musk and hammer away at myself

I craved clean semantics in a campaign mainland

And such spiritual insight that a god would even tie my shoes

I'm dressed like a Jamestown cannibal

In a city of mistake babies with e-cash

We all make mistakes

I don't need to tell you that

When I look up your life one day

A hypnotized life

I suppose there's a psychological reason for it

It's a hungry curtain that you close in your bedroom

And I'm on a sofa thinking of a friend

With her c-sectioned guts on a cold tray beside her

And me and Jon in my 240D

Cruising and disgusting

As if this weekend or any weekend can make the difference

Mezcal, Percocet in the leather booths

Every mortal swallowing for the same immortal reasons

I'd drive to a thousand Colorados to be free of instinct and urge

Spending my time with superlative killers

Poems just getting longer and inane

On summer afternoons

Children come out to pet the cop cars

In the park where Montgomery Clift is buried

I watch the Korean wedding parties

In the background of Korean wedding videos

You will find me sweating with my dog

On a night like this in July, Clift died in his bed

Around the corner was his favorite restaurant, The Isle of Capri

Serving a veal chop broiled to perfection

In the summer of the previous year I thought about Clift

When I was drinking in a Connecticut hotel

In a town known for its ballet dancers

Where I listed my dependencies to the labyrinthian wallpaper

Why do I now think of a friend years ago

Paid to water Jeff Koons' *Puppy* all summer

In its enormity

In its antigravity

Herzog said you can't answer a question like that with your shoes on

At times I dispatch an inward vision

And resign myself to free karma

Ladies and Gentleman

Let's look at you destroyed

I want to have your cremated freebies

Your passcodes whisper over the mountains

Of this round earth/abstract world

Where country music clichés

Burn steady into effervescence

VAGUE EFFICIENCY

I wasn't eager to find the ruins of a comb over

As a child I stuck my hands in bags of wet noodles

To learn our anatomy

Mom kept holy water in the spice rack

Our family grew closer with the death of an animal

Our family looked to a higher being for the light

The light that casts its cold shadows on birdbaths

The shadows in my forest of innuendoes

I'm so sorry significant others

This is not a resignation

The party in my brain is much too strong to wind down

This area is known as the zone-of-avoidance

A group of hot, young, bluish-white stars in the constellations

A jet engine's deep centrifuge over palladiums of art deco

I was sharing a ketchup bottle when I heard the R&B singer overdosed

I found calm in a seabed of ponytails at the parade

I contested a parking ticket

I fell asleep with a temporary tattoo

In the pale light of a savings bank

Well acquainted with the evil rub

That brings the machines to climax

PINNACLE MELTDOWN

I came here to write *The Jesus Poems*

Expel from youth the power to beautify waste

I'd drive through the Berkshires

The lights of the ski slope reflected off the overcast

I couldn't fight it anymore

My desire to generate laughter

I felt so in tune with my humor it kept me up at night

When I drive past a cemetery

I imagine all the metal screws and implants

Strewn in the ashy caskets

And I make a fully conscious effort

Not to think of hot widows

In tight black formal wear

Talking with frankness and freedom

About their slinky needs

I want to be alone with my browser searches

This machine humming like galvanized honeycomb

Taking advantage of the opulent core

At night I'd walk past the community college

And see the janitors reading the dry erase boards

I couldn't help being in love with the idea

All of our language there for the taking

Even handed out in a prospectus from a booth

A great satisfaction is reading from some unseen prompting machine

To a singular student body

The enchantment of an exhausted mirage

I come back to my hotel and run a bath of salt and lavender

I knew I had no grace when stepping out of the tub; I've no agility, no definition

Then I rummaged through my bag for my dark smoking shawl

What you do is hang one between your tropical shirt

And your three-piece herringbone

But in a casual kind of way

I was on so much Ativan

My expressions took on the tantrums of a squeezed parrot

It was in a New Mexico desert with a blown tire

Where I'd invented the solar-powered blowjob machine

And later, the wind-powered hand holder

(As I knew you were wondering how I could afford this time)

I continued work on *My Health is Good and My Financial Troubles are Over*

A love poem that had been haunting me

Resulting in goose bumps like an emotional Braille

I dreamt two locomotives advanced quickly towards one another

Each emblazoned with massive rococo mirrors

The wreckage was transformed into an exquisite shopping experience

A fashion period would be inspired from this called *Pinnacle Meltdown*

Everyone walked the streets looking as if pulled from earthquake rubble

I assure you these sensations will be obliterated from memory

On an afternoon walk to the outlet for sunglasses

Where residents form the sum of a paralyzing equation

In windbreakers dreaming a collective coupe

Like a postcard of a cruise ship taped to a prison cinderblock

You see teenage skyscrapers on the horizon

And one can't help but think of entrepreneurs

Eating macho candy bars

A cell phone vibrating a beach of desk pennies

A self-image no distance can cure

Like a photographer

You are not translating the world from scratch

Go meet the minimum requirements

Do it for the right reasons

Get on with showing your love already

ENTERPRISE

Through the plaza window
a tongue of waterfall

The river's mange

I'm in Niagara

Weather channel music

The casino

To be a better person
would be tremendous

_____

With a fever your head bobs and drains
in a new sundress
like a somnambulant germ

_____

Betwixt car dealerships

It's meatloaf night

I etch loins
with a toothpick
in the salt of a previous diner

Your ex bitched you out

I heard

———————————

Drought fields

Or an orphan pancake

Or an overturned baby's head filling with blood

———————————

In a dark bedroom

I know when your eyes are open

They emit a certain heat

———————————

Lonely swimmer

Kudzu jet skis

Beauteous snafus

Slander in the sand

With classy narcotics

With decorum

It's 'casual expensive'

Where we gossip

_____

Body claps echo

In the breezeway

Venetian slats of light

The arm hair is thick

The butt is flat

_____

Creaking down the beach house steps
with my cock

Burnished

Radiant

And vacationing

and I'd close my eyes and think about the sauce factory
and you'd know what time of day it was by the aroma
and everyone would be outside in hairnets smoking
and men would go by in motorized wheelchairs towards liquor stores
and some kids would be hanging off the back of them

_____

Enterprise

Satiated

Ersatz tombstone

Clandestine

At the apogee

_____

When your eyes dilate in the candlelit aura of top-forty

I consider if there is a safe and healthy dark without you

RARE AND SPECIAL INTERESTS

It's hard to explain
My ghost writing
When I remained
An insular entity
I came out of the dust
Looking like this
So I don't know
What's your story
I've some Jägermeister
A simple socialite
In a den of terracotta
If I sample all night your powders
And supply low-grade bios
To the bi-curious
I'd fail
To be the true adulterer I am
A lot of people say
Time will no longer tell
But public opinion is weird
True vice
Is understood without speaking

Under this rock is an answer
Under this car mat is a withered condom
One lake
Then two lakes
A wireless rainbow
A hotel of hands
Hands that presumably want
To inch towards an Eden
Where tunnels birth
Used Porsches
A monthly charitable donation
To a dead and marvelous love
A fresh ghost
Widowers must vacation from

The night I wanted your spouse
To do me a gloomy tax service
I negotiated a romance
To touch the loser
For your bravery test
Look at them
With enthusiasm
A patina of style debt
And cheap labor
They're harmless to resist
Like a dime on a lawn
Neighbors
Get out of my commercial
My environment is unique
My beaches are pink
As young brain matter
Like rival pathogens
I am the heir apparent
A cocktail predator
Your favorite uncle

These daily reflections
From cirrhosis of the Humors
To the dominos of Death
To finger the asshole of the muse
Is to risk discovering
What it eats
You're appealing to me
Reading this unpopular form of art
The work-late moms
The sort of gently Caribbean dads
Reaching through their binoculars
At the barnacles of zirconia
In the nose cartilage of
Those that take up the warm waters
Where we find ourselves
This afternoon
As blameless holy creatures

The body is a hothouse
A semi-soft, well-slept face
With the clouds half-dark
Like self-published authors
You crawl to your vacations
In the hallway
That Artforum is trying
To seduce your sister
The thuds and moans
In the next room
Sounds of tennis
The royal couple in attendance
It is kinda strange
He and she will die
At different times
For different reasons
As I continue to piss off Europe
Asleep on a Scottish hill
Desperate to be a genesis
Dying
Casually

What will happen

With an evil light

Like this

It'll come

Shining through on some

Slight clearances

Like promotional videos

On natural healing

Or sorority epitaphs

On heavy cotton

The palace purple

Gelatin capsules

Of antihistamine

Baby, I'm telling you

They dissolve

They wander

They get frisky

And I let them

Whilst lying beside this stone

Becoming a dopamine Christ

As a dozen sycamores

Police my anxiety

With fragrant breath

I'm now a tolerant

Son of a bitch

I don't like the way

The tree moves

But it moves

In my kiosk of self-love
I dream of a great reader's body
To compromise
In a cashmere of moods
A brilliant light
That vomits off the green
And dies in the shadows
My jellybean
My bonbon
Are you happy enough
To love everything you love
Everyone you love
With all your soft drinks
Staining the robotics
Of your vehicle
Towards a blanket area and sea reading
Applying superb ointments
Over blue-vein pale skin
The soft Russian art
Of your legs
Untroubled swans

How do you kill

A mountain of a man

But with a river of fries

Grass

Growing around the gurneys

Because the cancer patients

Are in hammocks

Allowing the fingers in a breeze

To play harps

On their areolas and scrotums

Maybe in the next life

You'll be a farm

And fear the tornado

Once again

I'll be a creep

That expunges the spirit

Gets consensual

With a neutered passion

Something living

That crept

Here is another example
You are not a twig
Endorsed by a conglomerate forest
To assassinate
The genuine guidance of nature
Nature is not cruel
It takes ideas to be cruel
In a two-way mirror
We are a benevolent haunting
In the speedboat
We console a crying friend
Lake water
Mussing the haircuts of babes
The moments we had in the sunlight
I'm like
Believe in me you pricks
Our duets are crystallized exhaust
Besotted
This can only last so long
I will miss people

Guess who's on an airplane
In the dark hum
Looking at the hotel pools
Lit below
And the pockets of white trash
Where actresses sometimes come from
Like Tammy
Who isn't an actress
But my neighbor that sunbathed
On the garage roof
Just outside my bedroom window
There still remains a desire
To see her next to a boombox
UV rays on her neckline
She has no idea what I've become
The tumor sized hell in my brain
That this color corrected flashback
Is being exploited for artistic use
By a petrified drunk
That only wants their precious ego
And this private event
Sustained

An entrepreneur

Sprucing up my face

Using a cream

Unbearably happy

With my membership to the Y

Seeking the non-poetic matter-of-facts

The outside world

Its temporary residence

In the blood

Heading to the fridge

During halftime

Unable to lack temptation

Of your designer mouth

As we kiss

Like a reluctant asteroid

Knowing at some point

It must destroy

Nothing personal
Glob of mercury
Molten spot of earth
The Nordstrom
The Bloomingdale
The placid pond
With many bodies
Baja rain shadows
In twin vapor
I'm in a grotto
Of self-worth
I'd like to thank
My friends
And editors
For my strident success
With humility
In the cloud-splattered orbit
Nothing is better
Nothing more personal
Than tranquil
Indifference

I've come to put to rest

My trusty medulla

And maybe

Yeah

In these sleazy conditions

My ideas need subtitles

Abstinent romances

Where we do our own mouths

But to court you

In this ugly shirt

To go between your legs

Like a fierce moon landing

I'd ignore

Baby-hungry flames

In an orphanage

To execute me

In slow motion

I savagely admit

My oscillating fears

Do I have regrets
Other than creating this portal
To a persistent moral scourge
The waterbed
As an idea
Never appealed to me
Can I massage your shoulders
While you enter your card number
Into a cursory field
Can I concede to a list of demands
Like wax
To vigorous treatment
I find myself in parks
At lunches
Fatalistic thresholds
Kissing foreheads
For fear of being
A crass totem
In the service of American Art
I push every kitten away
I couldn't be trusted

Sex Ed nostalgia
Ms. Cody
The jar between her legs
The whole sixth-grade class
One by one to her desk
Helena was the prettiest
But afterward
Her face was a dismal contortion
Then I stood from my seat
A fun fact about me is
I occasionally eat caviar
While watching sports networks
With the copper skies
Over the stadiums
The color of a fetus
Like in that jar
And this roe I enjoy
Is of no prior coincidence
Not a revenge

The smell of hay
And heavy chains
Get me so softcore
Denim
Alters an erection
I don't want to go
To the moon
I want to go
To a reasonable environment
Watching you touch yourself
In the duel pulsating jets
Don't say
This will never happen
I beg to balance
Our two options
Of the abyss
To Cinemax
Pour my liquor
Down your spine
Body butter me
I forget who wins

That caloric morsel

You ate in Yosemite

The sundry murders

You reminisce

Note the superstitious

Passively attractive sales rep

Note the artifact

Sexualized

By velvet ropes

I can tell

I can feel

Your orthodontic engines

Your sizzle of brass buttons

I'm standing with you

Your face is in a pie

Your hair has fallen out

From something

You ain't even heard of

You had a stroke

That's okay

But as a holistic gem

As a merciful tide

The glimmer I wear

From basins of touch screens

I put the rest of the death

In this poem

For you to finish

I know I talk
About these possessions
These slender affectionate souls
About standing cross-armed
At the museums
The darker pleasures
You must take me as genuine
It's truly the crematorium
The box of fire
The annihilating finality
I speak to
Am motivated by
This persona crumbles
My integrity pussyfoots
At times I sleep in beds
With rich partners
We are in a dark room
Wanting the same things
I'm not going to turn this around
And say I'm rich
Rich with poems
Because that is an early death
Like most of you
I don't want to die just yet
But I blow my brains out every day
That's what gets me out of bed
Searching for the reasons to

INFINITY POOL

When I look outside to the street, outside of my window with my sandwich
    in hand,
a cold sandwich, with triple-washed accoutrements the colors of third-world
    currency,
I wish to not subscribe to another magazine with politicians seated next to
    mugs of pens,
or ones that fetishize proteins glazed and accessorized.

When I'm on the elliptical I think about my blood test results.
And that I may be in love with the junkie eating her sandwich in the video at
    the museum.

I love going to museums and seeing the women and the thermo-hydrograph
    machines.
I love going to the museum and going out for fried chicken afterward.

When you are alone in a museum
you have no one hurting the accuracy of your recollections,
like how my parents had obviously rented their upstairs apartment
to an online prostitute. Or Brian taking those weekend trips to the state park
to masturbate in the shadow of a boulder, disturbed only once
by a hang glider walking out from behind some vegetation to the edge of the cliff.
Or when a friend was hitchhiking to Sag Harbor and got picked up by Billy Joel
but didn't know it was Billy Joel until they were already in town.
That summer I realized I had been shopping at the 7-Eleven
where the artist Ray Johnson parked his Volkswagen
before he drowned himself in the cove below the bridge.

Some think being an artist is a poor business model.
Still, I wouldn't mind being a business model.

There is a fine listener-supported rock station just north of the city.
I wasn't planning on talking about it
but *September Gurls* would be very favorable to hear
when looking out over the Hudson
because you are a vacationer
letting the paint dry on a still life of sports equipment.
And you are in an infinity pool.
And you are thinking of inventing a new perfume.
And the hills look like a burn victim, the barges
breaking the current with surplus, the reflection
of a hummingbird through your jalapeño vodka;
unequivocal creation with no perimeters.
For dessert; a little box of chocolate bunnies.
The sound of a mouth opening in an empty room.
Applying the pressure needed to bring its form to an end.

BON VOYAGE

Each morning a private ambition
A kind of material to deal with
To want leisure
To want carte blanche
A private ambition to spend
The rest of your days whipped
With licorice
To both suffer and enjoy the idea
That we aren't respectable
Your name so astral
In the dark
Corner of a home page
We're cultural wreckage
Fucked out
In this coastal spa
You tame my apnea
Your words
Cannot subterfuge
A mood ring
You ask for the sex towel
To wipe your chin
A private ambition
In humid decadence
On a docked boat
The nights so dark
A wet and sucking void
Esoteric things
Temporarily obtainable
Private ambitions

In order to see you again
I have to sleep
This
This is the stuff of the narcoleptic

COOL NEW FEAR

Mishandling of a delicate situation is somewhat of a turn on

I read about daily life bereft of reference points but surviving in practice

Like it's supposed to be some interesting post-mortem box set

The truth is I come home every night and botch an ideal solitary mystique

With an escalator for a nervous system

Perpetually tumbling a canvas sack of benzodiazepines

I am not interested in your writing about the Chateau Marmont

I am interested in the pigeons pecking at the puke of the party girl

I'm trying to keep this accessible for translation into major foreign languages

Like an animal's quest to solve an insignificant problem

It's the only way I'll phoenix

I am forced to love life or suffer the pleasure of not caring

Staring at a marble pyramid on an onyx coffee table

Unmarred by so much work of delusion

I'm looking for a streamlined artistically-styled peace

Placing yourself in a poem is martyrdom

It comes from an anxiety that death feels like eternal blue balls

I apologize if I evoke a cool new fear

Searching for a single visible object to embody public virtue

Like chakras dipped in chocolate

Like songbirds on the chiseled forearm of a mute

On what I believe is the gilded rubric

Lest the lousy stone on a mesa

Vandalize the temple of a non-believer

Though murder is passé

Someone has had to die in order to know

What to eat or how to sail

I wanted to be your trinity maker

But it's the promises that are keeping me delinquent

And you've already failed me

There're artists and stuff everywhere

Famous in their transparent malaise

And I fear I simply cannot hold this pose a second longer

SNOBS

It is rare people make any appearance in these collected works

Though it is people who love access to prohibited areas

Everyone lives to love but continually dreams to kill

SECONDARY MONSTER

After swim class I look in the mirror and I still am nothing

You don't want to drown at the wrong party

Or watch the coral pink jet streams mar the sunset

From a gazebo waiting for your father to die

Some test at destroying an object's utility

You have a lewd experience in a maritime sweater

Midnight waves like a dozen wedding gowns tumbling toward you

Confess your super dreams to the rich and murky smear of cake

The days of buying a car on looks alone are over

We shoot anise liquors from the tombs of a total dive

We go out to nightclubs with music from Saudi Arabia

Take a hundred photographs of a foot bathed in a tulip bed

Everything in soft-focus but a seductive soapy hand

The shadow of a bird like a thrown hammer

A butterfly released from a cargo pocket

Little boutique salvations commanding issues on the wild afterlife

The lake encasing you in its natural mirror

With your pantyhose like snakeskin in a tuft of leaves

A horsefly taking its time in your hair

LEGAL / TENDER

More or less aroused in a damp vista

We broke out with civic glory stressing any awareness of this condition

Axioms like an outdoorsy surrogate parent

Knowing that Churchill had been born in the ladies room during a dance

Flanked by a decorative ice eagle

And pictures of children in anniversary war paints

I work the Steel Magnolias angle

Crying about sickness past the doorman

Pick up a flashlight and turn it on

The heart of the switch touched by a complicit finger

Cunnilingus to the keyhole, fondle the deadbolt

Who was I fooling; I was an atheist who couldn't stop touching himself

I've returned to the point of no return

Through the peephole you are wrapped in a dreamy light

You are bound and gagged and I accept that

By bound and gagged I mean, how much longer are you going to read

I watch the seconds on my wrist form out of liquid crystal

Reason shattering into place

Many important people have trusted me with their plants and dogs

MOOD LIGHTING

We waited in the even mellow light for the doorbell
Someone whispered, *positive vibes, positive vibes*
I'm not exactly a master
I'm not even in séance mode
Channeling the isolated spirit of a marble on a fox rug
I want purity moments
My interests are a combination of mood lighting
And exotic materials
This is where I alpha
Over envisioned bramble
We move in pursuit like cop boats
Through boring flowerbeds
Through Halls of Fame
In streets with pomade
Walking hand in hand past stands of ghetto films
A waitress brings us goods from a roadhouse menu
There is a child with a hairlip scar like a capo
Begging for a poorly propelled coin
That child will go on to own a blood bank
In a town modeled on nurse dreams
Arts and Ministry
Sports and Medicine
The eventual, spawning endlessly
We take to the beaches
A kind of lubed ordnance
With ergonomic crucifixes
Your Honor, I present the last donut
Filled with superior color
And I prepare to speak to you
A breath mint pertinent on the tongue

Allowing the fact there is taco on my corduroy

I'd consider saying you're a portable energy

Held accountable

In a cascading cud

I've succumbed to

I'm the other woman

Your claimed bitch

Used for inspiration

My munitions of liquor

And penultimate lovemaking

I'm willing to be enticed

You can entice me

As I get in touch with my antimatter

And chant for temperance

In and out of napping

Via waves of cold energy drink

I come as arson

As an amphitheater of nylon

It is not so hard

To accept meaninglessness

Acceptance is very meaningful

One quantum chain of ganglia

Not to necessarily fix

But eventually adapt

LIQUID ASSETS

The civic purposes of the museum, were not to be a "mere cabinet of curiosities
which serve to kill time for the idle" but instead "tend directly to humanize,
to educate and refine a practical and laborious people."

Pork into porcelain.

This is 1880 at The Metropolitan Museum of Art.

The museum developed a snobbish reputation.

It was argued the museum could aid in the "struggle against gigantic vices,"
and to elevate the retrograde.

These particulars are in effect an acid wash over the vulgar breadth of expertise.

I know many people living lives of artistic practice
that cannot take care of themselves,
and not out of paraplegic circumstance.

Art has not refined them.

They are porcelain.

Success, today, is the progressive realization of an ideal within a bubble.

I want to go to the biennial anyway.

We exist in postures.

We don't need an intensive course in anatomy
to lay our hands on another human being.

Touch your partner while you read this.

All of us sufficient actors with zero nostalgia.

And this is the mirror we've looked for.

A gnarled buddy system to analyze our sentient world.

Poised, chill, and alone.

But oh that ass, honey.

Limitations, it seems, give people who accomplish nothing satisfaction.
David Copperfield covered a $60,000 Ferrari with a large cloth
and with his gestures he slowly ascended it towards the rafters.
This took place against a sequin backdrop with skyscraper silhouettes.
After disproving the possibility of attachments
with a sharp pull the cloth came away.
To the disappointment of some
the Ferrari had vanished.

"At the museum I look at people with the eyes of an artist, in the street with my own."

This is Edouard Levé.

Also, "contradicting myself brings two kinds of pleasure: betraying myself and having a new opinion."

Every new generation achieves its character through acting out the fantasies of the previous one.

Modern youths are still lonely.

But love—they have found it—in their own reflections.

We are clearly on this plateau.

Think about the quality of a free opera.

A psychic event waving our hands around polygon temples.

Easing on.

An everlasting ammunition.

There is no use for prayer if you alone exist.

Narcissism is like a cliff shrub easily giving way to gentle pressure.

Like a director looked into our dreams.

Doing nothing, but doing it well.

The same monetary note used for both deplorable and charitable acts is transubstantiated through moral intervention.

(a) Fuck.
(b) Fuck yes.

Money has no conscience.

It's a frothy matter that stokes young criminal emotions.

Hold a cheap pearl tightly in your hand and visualize money flowing into your life. Now throw the pearl into an ocean or stream. If you cannot find an ocean or stream simply throw it into a mound of trash. The act of sympathetic magic will still manifest your desired condition.

"I got burned up by vanity and folly."

This is Eve Babitz.

Cigar ash ignited her skirt whilst driving home from a Hollywood party.

She claimed to have suffered from "squalid overboogie."

This physical fact reduces to psychological effect.

She remains secluded in her alien world,
the rest existing for us.

Abject Class: A cocktail of all the remnant liquors in the home.

The drink being consistently different, the taste being more of a lifestyle.

And one is not being charged with the same crime twice.

Ask Americans to crack a window for the fashion burger.

Fog machines help present you with your new kidney.

The reality of chemistry is that the fame of urine as fluid
is only next to the fame of blood.

Water remaining in dead fountains is also symbiotic.

Nature never giving up—try and imagine another place.

Yes, you will still get your ocean.

We're not unable to accommodate that.

How the sunlight lands just so on the taint.

You make the songs follow wherever you go.

Beginners, please.

We don't need a good line anymore.

This is the contemporary art we've been meaning to get into.

Fluid as hell.

NOTIONS OF PARADISE

If I was to be a conceptual star I needed space
My bank teller, my service provider, my general practitioner
They are all aware of my limitations
At night dream rubble entombs me
With utterances of incandescent wisdom
From behind a detective's glass door
It'd be safer to leave the celebrity
Of briefly handling the biographies of show dogs
In beige fantasies
Thousands of years before my creations found a medium

Around the home you'll find battery-powered fragrances

Hot appliances

Soft rubber aerobic pads in various glows

I watched the antacid cyclones in her tap water

Hearing about the dinner in detail

Our friend had oversaturated the market

With his pregnant lizard paintings

My mind drifted into the loafers

Of a substitute teacher

As caves of second-rate attraction

Frequenting the same container of love hoping to find

The contents drastically changed

What made the drinking so good was the erasure

On cold nights with the bar windows body humid and dripping

It is a mistake for you to think you are the only one

The only one that can drive with panache through the abbreviated beauty

Diplomas, diplomas, diplomas,

The wind in the nearby hospital trees

A spirit rising from black sweatpants

Like Freud's death train wheezing in the sparse heather

With poems equal in weight to an urn of third mind paradise
Poems equal in weight to an urn of tornado grass
Poems equal in weight to an urn of debutante hands
I will write poems equal in weight to an urn of eastern law firms
Often leaving them in the welcome binders of hotels

Then we'd go see the Nudes
Bruised Cash
Fraught Lasers
Chinatown Sunlight
Catamarans
Beer Memorabilia
Country Exquisites
Devices that Soothe

And I'd wave to the brunch people

And I'd read about Bolivia's lithium

And I'd glance at the antiquities of public waste management in collegiate texts

And I think of you lacquered in a Pompeii of dance light

Surrounded by squadrons of beauty

This was weeks after our dog walker's suicide

In the morning, touching your phone in bed

Our toothbrushes in essential but largely sexless bliss

To hear the primordial drop on a pregnancy test

Massive negotiating silence

Space

This space

A collection of space

That I curate

Where I forgive myself

ACKNOWLEDGEMENTS

The author wishes to acknowledge the editors of
the following publications in which some of these poems
first appeared: *Boston Review, The Brooklyn Rail, Fence,
jubilat, The Minus Times, Prelude, Sixth Finch,* and *TRNSFR.*

Some of the work was originally published in two
limited-edition chapbooks, *Legal Pure* (Greying Ghost
Press, 2012) and *From the Author's Private Collection*
(The Song Cave, 2013).

The author would like to thank John Ashbery, Ben Fain,
Betsey Fortlouis, Matt LaFleur, Monica McClure,
Emily Skillings, Sampson Starkweather, Chris Tonelli,
and Birds, LLC. To Michele Mortimer, with gratitude.

Eric Amling (b.1981) lives and works in New York City.

His work has been exhibited in various cities
in the United States. This is his debut collection.

"POETRY, LIKE CAT URINE, CAN RUIN THE INTEGRITY OF A ROOM," WRITES ERIC AMLING, BUT "IT CAN ALSO BE A STEALTHY DOMINATRIX." IT IS AND DOES BOTH IN THESE STARTLED, SUBVERSIVE POEMS, WHICH CHURN UP A DISORDERED GLEE. BUT IT'S REASSURING TO KNOW THAT "ALL OF THESE WORKS WILL BE FILED IN A CUSTOM MATRIX/ APPROVED BY THIRD-TIER ANALYSTS/ IN A HALL OF DUELING NATIONAL ANTHEMS."

— JOHN ASHBERY